WORKBOOK

For

The New Model of Selling

Selling to an Unsellable Generation

[A Comprehensive Guide To implementing

Jerry Acuff and Jeremy Miner 's Book]

Dunne Press

This workbook is intended to be used as a companion to the book. While it can be utilized independently, it is designed to enhance the reader's experience and understanding of the concepts presented in the book. This workbook is not intended to replace or serve as a substitute for the original book.

Table of Content

How To Use This Workbook

Welcome to the companion workbook for **The New Model of Selling: Selling to an Unsellable Generation** by Jerry Acuff and Jeremy Miner. This workbook is designed to help you dive deeper into the content of the original book and apply its principles to your life. Here's how to use this book:

Overview

The workbook starts with a general summary of the original book, which provides an overview of the key themes and concepts.

Chapter Sections

Each chapter in the workbook includes the following sections:

- Summary: A brief summary of the chapter's content.
- Key Lessons: A list of the key lessons from the chapter.
- Self-Reflection Questions: A list of questions designed to help you reflect on the chapter's content and apply it to your life.
- Action Steps: A list of practical steps you can take to apply the chapter's content to your life.

Learning Review Questions

At the end of the workbook, there is a section of Learning Review questions. These questions are designed to help you review and reinforce the key concepts from the book. You can use these questions to test your understanding of the material and identify areas where you may need to review or study further.

To get the most out of this workbook, we recommend the following:

- Read the overview of the original book before starting the workbook.
- Read each chapter of the workbook carefully, taking notes as needed.
- Complete the self-reflection questions for each chapter, taking time to reflect on your answers.
- Use the action steps to apply the chapter's content to your life.
- Review the Learning Review questions at the end of the workbook to reinforce your understanding of the material.

Overview

Jerry Acuff and Jeremy Miner's book "The New Model of Marketing: Selling to an Unsellable Generation" discusses the obstacles and techniques for marketing to the present generation, which is frequently viewed as "unsellable". The writers dive into the traits and interests of this generation, presenting insights and ways to successfully engage and convince them.

The book opens by analyzing the shifting environment of sales and how conventional selling approaches are no longer successful in gaining the attention and interest of the unsellable generation. Acuff and Miner claim that this generation is very suspicious and resistant to conventional sales approaches, making it vital for sales professionals to modify their approach.

One significant topic underlined in the book is the importance of creating trust with clients. The writers underline that trust is the cornerstone of effective marketing in today's market. They give practical tips on how to develop trust, such as actively listening to consumers, understanding their requirements, and delivering on commitments.

Furthermore, the book investigates the role of technology in contemporary sales. Acuff and Miner admit that technology has revolutionized the way consumers acquire goods and services.

They examine how sales professionals may harness technology to strengthen their selling process, including employing social media platforms, online reviews, and targeted marketing methods.

Another key issue explored in the book is the value of narrative in sales. The authors suggest that narrative is a great technique for connecting consumers emotionally and generating a memorable experience. They give examples and advice on how to write captivating tales that appeal to the unsellable generation.

Additionally, The New Model of Selling stresses the significance of constant learning and self-improvement for sales professionals. Acuff and Miner emphasize that being informed of market developments, refining communication skills, and having a growth mentality are key to success in selling to an unsellable generation.

In conclusion, the book provides significant insights and techniques for sales professionals attempting to manage the problems of selling to the present generation. It highlights the necessity of creating trust, utilizing technology, storytelling, and continual learning in order to successfully engage and convince the unsellable generation.

The Biggest Problems in Sales

Summary

Jeremy Miner highlight the largest challenge in sales today: the unsellable generation. The authors believe that the old approach to selling, which included the salesman convincing the consumer to purchase a product or service, is no longer successful since buyers today are more knowledgeable and suspicious than ever before.

Key Lessons

- The old approach to selling is no longer successful.
- Customers nowadays are more knowledgeable and suspicious than ever before.
- The unsellable generation is the largest difficulty in sales today.
- The unsellable generation is not interested in being sold to but instead wants to make educated selections based on value and trust.
- Sales professionals must adapt to the requirements of the unsellable generation to be successful.
- Building connections and giving value are important to marketing to the unsellable generation.
- The new approach to selling focuses on creating connections, understanding client requirements, and giving value that fits those needs.

Self-Reflection Questions

How have you altered your sales technique to address the demands of the unsellable generation?

_____

_____

_____

_____

_____

_____

_____

_____

_____

_____

_____

Do you emphasize creating connections with clients in your sales process?

_____

_____

_____

_____

_____

_____

_____

_____

_____

_____

_____

_____

How do you convey the value of your product or service to customers?

_____

_____

_____

_____

_____

_____

_____

_____

_____

_____

_____

_____

Are you able to comprehend and handle the requirements
and issues of your customers?

_____

_____

_____

_____

_____

_____

_____

_____

_____

_____

_____

How do you develop trust with customers in your sales process?

_____

_____

_____

_____

_____

_____

_____

_____

_____

_____

Are you open to learning new sales strategies and approaches to adapt to the changing market?

_____

_____

_____

_____

Action Steps

- Research and learn about the requirements and concerns of the unsellable generation.
- Focus on creating connections with consumers rather than simply completing a transaction.
- Understand the value of your product or service and convey it effectively to consumers.
- Listen to consumers and ask questions to obtain a better grasp of their wants and issues.
- Build trust with consumers by being honest, truthful, and dependable.
- Seek out training and coaching to improve your sales talents and adapt to the changing market.

Sales Myths versus Sales Realities

Summary

Jerry Acuff and Jeremy Miner refute various sales fallacies and emphasize the reality of selling in the current world. The authors suggest that many old sales tactics are no longer effective and that sales professionals must adapt to the changing market to be successful.

Key Lessons

- Many classic sales methods are no longer effective.
- Sales personnel must adapt to the changing market to be successful.
- Building connections and offering value are more essential than persuasion in marketing today.
- Customers nowadays are more aware and want to make informed selections based on value and trust.
- The emphasis of selling has changed from the product to the client and their requirements.
- The sales process is no longer linear but is now a continual cycle of creating connections, giving value, and nurturing the client.
- Sales personnel must be informed about their product or service and its value to the consumer.

Self-Reflection Questions

Do you depend on old sales tactics, or do you adapt to the changing market to be successful?

_____

_____

_____

_____

_____

_____

_____

_____

_____

_____

How do you develop connections with clients in your sales process?

_____

_____

_____

_____

_____

_____

_____

_____

_____

_____

_____

Are you able to deliver value to consumers that fits their requirements and challenges?

_____

_____

_____

_____

_____

_____

_____

_____

_____

_____

_____

_____

How do you convey the value of your product or service to customers?

_____

_____

_____

_____

_____

_____

_____

_____

_____

_____

_____

Have you changed your attention from the product to the client and their requirements in your sales approach?

_____

_____

_____

_____

_____

_____

_____

_____

_____

_____

_____

Are you able to continue a constant cycle of creating connections, giving value, and nurturing the customer?

_____

_____

_____

_____

_____

_____

_____

_____

_____

_____

_____

_____

_____

Action Steps

- Evaluate your sales methods and discover any typical practices that may no longer be productive.
- Focus on creating connections with clients and offering value that fits their requirements.
- Invest time in learning about your consumers and their issues to better understand their demands.
- Communicate the value of your product or service in a manner that connects with the consumer.
- Shift your attention from the product to the client and their requirements in your sales technique.
- Develop a continual cycle of creating connections, giving value, and nurturing the consumer.

Unlocking the Gatekeepers

Summary

The authors examine the necessity of unlocking gatekeepers in the sales process. They claim that gatekeepers, such as receptionists and assistants, may be crucial influences in the decision-making process and should not be disregarded by sales professionals.

Key Lessons

- Gatekeepers may be major influences in the decision-making process.
- Gatekeepers should not be disregarded by sales professionals.
- Building connections with gatekeepers may help open doors to decision-makers.
- Gatekeepers may provide vital information about the decision-making process and the demands of the client.
- Treating gatekeepers with respect and professionalism may help develop trust and rapport.
- Sales personnel should not underestimate the impact of gatekeepers in the sales process.
- The new approach to selling stresses creating connections with all stakeholders, including gatekeepers.

Self-Reflection Questions

Do you neglect gatekeepers in the sales process, or do you acknowledge their importance?

_____

_____

_____

_____

_____

_____

_____

_____

_____

_____

_____

How do you create connections with gatekeepers in your sales process?

_____

_____

_____

_____

_____

_____

_____

_____

_____

_____

_____

_____

Are you able to obtain important information about the decision-making process and the demands of the client from gatekeepers?

_____

_____

_____

_____

_____

_____

_____

_____

_____

_____

_____

_____

_____

Do you handle gatekeepers with respect and professionalism in your contacts with them?

_____

_____

_____

_____

_____

_____

_____

_____

_____

_____

_____

_____

Have you ever misjudged the influence of gatekeepers in the sales process?

_____

_____

_____

_____

_____

_____

_____

_____

_____

_____

Do you emphasize creating connections with all stakeholders, including gatekeepers, in your sales approach?

_____

_____

_____

_____

_____

_____

_____

_____

_____

_____

_____

_____

Action Steps

- Recognize the role of gatekeepers in the sales process and make a deliberate effort to interact with them.
- Build connections with gatekeepers by showing an interest in their job and duties.
- Ask gatekeepers for their ideas and insights on the decision-making process and the demands of the consumer.
- Treat gatekeepers with respect and professionalism in all encounters.
- Don't underestimate the importance of gatekeepers in the sales process; understand their significance.

Getting Customer-Focused

Summary

Jerry Acuff and Jeremy Miner underline the significance of being customer-focused in the sales process. The authors suggest that effective sales professionals put the demands and difficulties of the client at the forefront of their approach and personalize their solutions appropriately.

Key Lessons

- Successful sales professionals place the demands and difficulties of the client at the center of their strategy.
- Consumer-focused selling requires listening, understanding, and reacting to the demands of the consumer.
- Sales personnel must be informed about their customers industries, difficulties, and ambitions.
- Building connections and trust are important to customer-focused selling.
- Sales professionals must be able to express the value of their product or service in a manner that connects with the consumer.
- A customer-focused sales technique entails a constant cycle of listening, learning, and reacting to the demands of the consumer.

Self-Reflection Questions

Do you place the wants and difficulties of the client at the center of your sales approach?

_____

_____

_____

_____

_____

_____

_____

_____

_____

_____

How do you listen to and comprehend the demands of the customer?

_____

_____

_____

_____

_____

_____

_____

_____

_____

_____

_____

_____

Are you informed about your customer's industry, difficulties, and goals?

_____

_____

_____

_____

_____

_____

_____

_____

_____

_____

_____

_____

How can you develop connections and trust with clients in your sales process?

_____

_____

_____

_____

_____

_____

_____

_____

_____

_____

Are you able to explain the value of your product or service effectively to customers?

_____

_____

_____

_____

_____

_____

_____

_____

_____

_____

How can you enhance your customer-focused approach in the sales process?

_____

_____

_____

_____

_____

_____

_____

_____

_____

_____

_____

_____

Action Steps

- Prioritize the wants and difficulties of the consumer in your sales technique.
- Listen carefully to consumers and ask questions to understand their requirements and concerns.
- Research and learn about your customer's industry, difficulties, and aspirations to better understand their requirements.
- Build connections and trust with consumers by being honest, upfront, and dependable.
- Communicate the value of your product or service in a manner that connects with the consumer.
- Seek input from consumers to strengthen your customer-focused approach and provide greater value.

Using the Power of Your Voice

Summary

This chapter highlights the necessity of leveraging the power of your voice in the sales process. The authors suggest that strong communication skills, including tone, tempo, and intonation, may assist sales professionals in creating trust and rapport with consumers and eventually completing more transactions.

Key Lessons

- Effective communication skills are crucial in the sales process.
- Tone, tempo, and inflection may impact how the consumer sees the sales professional and their message.
- Sales personnel must be able to adjust their communication approach to the demands and preferences of the consumer.
- Nonverbal communication, such as body language and facial emotions, can play a part in efficient communication.
- Sales professionals must be confident and forceful in their interactions, but also compassionate and knowledgeable of the customer's demands.
- Active listening is vital to good communication and helps create trust and connection with the consumer.

Self-Reflection Questions

How do you employ tone, tempo, and inflection in your conversation with customers?

_____

_____

_____

_____

_____

_____

_____

_____

_____

_____

_____

Are you able to modify your communication style to meet the demands and preferences of the customer?

_____

_____

_____

_____

_____

_____

_____

_____

_____

_____

_____

_____

How do you employ nonverbal communication, such as body language and facial emotions, in the sales process?

_____

_____

_____

_____

_____

_____

_____

_____

_____

_____

_____

_____

Are you confident and forceful in your conversations while still being compassionate and mindful of the customer's needs?

_____

_____

_____

_____

_____

_____

_____

_____

_____

_____

_____

Do you employ active listening in your conversations with customers?

_____

_____

_____

_____

_____

_____

_____

_____

_____

_____

How can you enhance your communication abilities to develop stronger connections and complete more deals?

_____

_____

_____

_____

_____

_____

_____

_____

_____

_____

_____

_____

Action Steps

- Practice utilizing tone, tempo, and inflection to deliver your point effectively.
- Adapt your communication approach to the demands and tastes of the consumer.
- Use nonverbal communication, such as body language and facial expressions, to support your message and develop connection.
- Be bold and aggressive in your discussions while still being compassionate and knowledgeable of the customer's demands.
- Embrace active listening to better grasp the customer's requirements and concerns.
- Seek feedback on your communication style and make modifications to improve it.

Listen and Learn

Summary

In this chapter, the authors highlight the significance of listening and learning in the sales process. They suggest that sales professionals who take the time to really understand the wants and difficulties of the client are better positioned to deliver solutions that fulfill their demands and eventually complete more transactions.

Key Lessons

- Listening is a vital skill in the sales process.
- Effective listening entails being present and totally interested in the discourse.
- Salespeople must be ready to ask questions and delve further to genuinely grasp the demands and issues of the consumer.
- Sales personnel must be open-minded and eager to learn from the customer's viewpoint.
- The new model of selling stresses the significance of listening and learning in the sales process.
- Salespeople who take the time to really understand the customer's wants and issues are better positioned to propose solutions that suit their demands and ultimately complete more transactions.

Self-Reflection Questions

Are you totally present and engaged in talks with customers?

_____

_____

_____

_____

_____

_____

_____

_____

_____

_____

Do you ask questions and delve deeper to genuinely grasp the wants and issues of the customer?

_____

_____

_____

_____

_____

_____

_____

_____

_____

_____

_____

Are you actively listening to develop trust and rapport with the customer?

_____

_____

_____

_____

_____

_____

_____

_____

_____

_____

_____

Do you approach interactions with an open mind and an eagerness to learn from the customer's perspective?

_____

_____

_____

_____

_____

_____

_____

_____

_____

_____

_____

How can you enhance your listening abilities in the sales process?

_____

_____

_____

_____

_____

_____

_____

_____

_____

_____

Are you willing to acknowledge when you don't know something and seek clarification from the customer?

_____

_____

_____

_____

_____

_____

_____

_____

_____

_____

_____

_____

_____

Action Steps

- Practice being totally present and involved in talks with consumers.
- Ask inquiries and delve further to genuinely grasp the demands and difficulties of the consumer.
- Practice active listening to create trust and rapport with the consumer.
- Approach interactions with an open mind and an eagerness to learn from the customer's viewpoint.
- Take notes throughout interactions to better grasp the customer's wants and issues.
- Admit when you don't know anything and seek clarification from the consumer.

Sequence of Questions

Summary

Jerry Acuff and Jeremy Miner address the value of employing a succession of questions in the sales process. The authors suggest that asking the correct questions in the proper sequence might help salespeople better grasp the wants and difficulties of the client and eventually complete more transactions.

Key Lessons

- A succession of inquiries may help salespeople better grasp the wants and issues of the client.
- Effective questioning entails asking open-ended questions that enable the consumer to give their opinion.
- Sales personnel must listen intently and ask follow-up questions to clarify and enhance their grasp of the customer's demands.
- The appropriate sequence of inquiries may help salespeople find the fundamental cause of the customer's difficulties and give more effective solutions.
- Professionals must be cautious of the timing and tempo of their queries to prevent overloading or aggravating the consumer.

Self-Reflection Questions

Do you employ a succession of questions in the sales process?

_____

_____

_____

_____

_____

_____

_____

_____

_____

_____

_____

Are you asking open-ended questions that enable the consumer to offer their perspective?

_____

_____

_____

_____

_____

_____

_____

_____

_____

_____

_____

Are you actively listening and asking follow-up questions to clarify and enhance your grasp of the customer's needs?

_____

_____

_____

_____

_____

_____

_____

_____

_____

_____

_____

_____

How can you enhance your questioning style to better identify the core cause of the customer's challenges?

_____

_____

_____

_____

_____

_____

_____

_____

_____

_____

_____

Are you attentive to the timing and tempo of your queries throughout the sales process?

_____

_____

_____

_____

_____

_____

_____

_____

_____

_____

How can you better incorporate a series of questions into your sales approach?

_____

_____

_____

_____

_____

_____

_____

_____

_____

_____

_____

_____

_____

Action Steps

- Develop a series of open-ended questions to utilize in the sales process.
- Practice active listening and asking follow-up questions to enhance your grasp of the customer's demands.
- Adjust your series of questions depending on the customer's replies to better grasp their difficulties and requirements.
- Be cautious of the timing and tempo of your queries to prevent overloading or aggravating the consumer.
- Continuously modify and change your sequence of questions depending on comments and experience.

To Sell or not to sell? That is the Question

Summary

In this chapter, the authors examine the significance of balancing the drive to sell with the need to create connections with clients. The authors claim that sales professionals who emphasize creating trust and rapport with consumers are better positioned to complete agreements in the long term.

Key Lessons

- Building connections with customers is crucial in the sales process.
- Sales professionals must be ready to walk away from a sale if it's not in the best interest of the consumer.
- Sales personnel must combine the impulse to sell with the requirement to create trust and connection with consumers.
- The new style of selling stresses the significance of creating connections with consumers above short-term purchases.
- Sales personnel must be truthful and honest with the consumer to develop trust and confidence.
- The new paradigm of selling stresses the necessity of becoming a trusted adviser to the consumer.

Self-Reflection Questions

Do you value creating connections with clients above short-term sales?

_____

_____

_____

_____

_____

_____

_____

_____

Are you prepared to walk away from a contract if it's not in the best interest of the customer?

_____

_____

_____

_____

_____

_____

_____

_____

_____

_____

_____

Are you straightforward and honest with consumers to develop trust and credibility?

_____

_____

_____

_____

_____

_____

_____

_____

_____

_____

_____

_____

How can you better present yourself as a trusted adviser
to the customer?

_____

_____

_____

_____

_____

_____

_____

_____

_____

_____

_____

Do you concentrate on developing long-term connections with clients rather than short-term sales?

_____

_____

_____

_____

_____

_____

_____

_____

_____

_____

Are you prepared to put the customer's requirements ahead of your ambition to clinch a deal?

_____

_____

_____

_____

_____

_____

_____

_____

_____

_____

_____

_____

Action Steps

- Prioritize creating connections with clients above short-term revenue.
- Be prepared to walk away from a contract if it's not in the best interest of the consumer.
- Be truthful and honest with consumers to develop trust and confidence.
- Position yourself as a valued adviser to the customer by delivering value and insights.
- Focus on creating long-term connections with clients rather than short-term revenue.
- Put the customer's requirements ahead of your ambition to seal a sale.
- Continuously concentrate on creating connections with consumers and being a trusted authority in your field.

The Engagement Stage

Summary

This chapter address the significance of the engagement stage in the sales process. The authors suggest that the engagement stage is crucial in creating trust and rapport with consumers and setting the scene for a successful sales result.

Key Lessons

- The engagement stage is crucial to creating trust and rapport with clients.
- Sales personnel must be sincere and genuine in their dealings with consumers.
- Effective engagement entails actively listening and asking questions to understand the customer's requirements and concerns.
- Salespeople must deliver value and insights to the client at the engagement stage.
- The engagement stage sets the groundwork for a good sales result.
- The new model of selling highlights the significance of the engagement stage in the sales process.
- Salespeople who perform well in the engagement stage are better able to create long-term connections with clients.

Self-Reflection Questions

Are you sincere and genuine in your contacts with clients at the engagement stage?

_____

_____

_____

_____

_____

_____

_____

_____

_____

_____

_____

Do you actively listen and ask questions to understand the customer's requirements and challenges?

_____

_____

_____

_____

_____

_____

_____

_____

_____

_____

_____

_____

How can you deliver additional value and insights to the consumer at the engagement stage?

_____

_____

_____

_____

_____

_____

_____

_____

_____

_____

_____

_____

Are you laying the groundwork for a great sales result during the engagement stage?

_____

_____

_____

_____

_____

_____

_____

_____

_____

_____

How can you better integrate the new model of selling into your approach during the engagement stage?

_____

_____

_____

_____

_____

_____

_____

_____

_____

_____

Are you creating trust and rapport with consumers throughout the engagement stage?

_____

_____

_____

_____

_____

_____

_____

_____

_____

_____

_____

_____

Action Steps

- Be true and sincere in your interactions with clients throughout the engagement stage.
- Practice active listening and asking questions to understand the customer's requirements and concerns.
- Provide value and insights to the consumer at the engagement stage.
- Set the stage for a good sales result during the engagement stage.
- Incorporate the new paradigm of selling into your approach throughout the engagement stage.
- Focus on creating trust and rapport with consumers throughout the engagement stage.

The Transitional Stage

Summary

Jerry Acuff and Jeremy Miner cover the transitional stage, which is the stage of the sales process when the consumer changes from being a prospect to a client. The writers underline the need to establish a seamless transition from the engagement stage to the transitional period to achieve a good sales result.

Key Lessons

- The transitional stage is the step of the sales process when the customer changes from being a prospect to a client.
- Effective transitional communication entails being precise and succinct in your message.
- Sales professionals must articulate the value proposition and advantages of their solution throughout the transitional period.
- The transitional period is a time to resolve any objections or issues the consumer may have.
- Sales personnel must be proactive in their communication throughout the changeover period.
- The new model of selling highlights the significance of establishing a seamless transition from the engagement stage to the transitional period.

Self-Reflection Questions

Are you precise and straightforward in your communications throughout the changeover stage?

_____

_____

_____

_____

_____

_____

_____

_____

_____

_____

_____

Are you successfully articulating the value proposition and advantages of your solution throughout the transitional stage?

_____

_____

_____

_____

_____

_____

_____

_____

_____

_____

_____

How do you handle complaints or issues the consumer may have during the changeover stage?

_____

_____

_____

_____

_____

_____

_____

_____

_____

_____

_____

_____

Are you proactive in your communication throughout the changeover stage?

_____

_____

_____

_____

_____

_____

_____

_____

_____

_____

_____

How can you strengthen your transitional communication to enable a seamless shift from prospect to client?

_____

_____

_____

_____

_____

_____

_____

_____

_____

_____

Are you efficiently exploiting the transitional period to develop long-term connections with customers?

_____

_____

_____

_____

_____

_____

_____

_____

_____

_____

_____

_____

_____

Action Steps

- Develop a clear and succinct message during the transitional time.
- Communicate the value proposition and advantages of your solution throughout the transitional period.
- Be prepared to answer any complaints or issues the consumer may have throughout the transitioning time.
- Be proactive in your communication throughout the transitioning era.
- Use the transitional period to create long-term connections with clients.
- Incorporate the new model of selling into your approach throughout the transitional period.

The Commitment Stage

Summary

This chapter explores the commitment stage, which is the ultimate step of the sales process. The writers underline the necessity of obtaining commitment from the consumer and facilitating a seamless transition to the post-sale relationship.

Key Lessons

- Salespeople who perform well in the commitment stage are better positioned to create long-term connections with clients.
- The commitment stage is the last step of the sales process.
- Sales professionals must properly convey the terms and conditions of the transaction at the commitment stage.
- The commitment stage is a time to address any last objections or issues the consumer may have.
- Sales professionals must facilitate a seamless transition to the post-sale relationship during the commitment stage.
- The new paradigm of selling stresses the necessity of obtaining commitment from the consumer.
- Sales personnel must be tenacious in their quest for commitment from the consumer.

Self-Reflection Questions

How can you successfully convey the terms and conditions of the sale at the commitment stage?

_____

_____

_____

_____

_____

_____

_____

_____

_____

_____

How do you handle any last objections or issues the consumer may have at the commitment stage?

_____

_____

_____

_____

_____

_____

_____

_____

_____

_____

_____

_____

Are you facilitating a seamless transition to the post-sale relationship during the commitment stage?

_____

_____

_____

_____

_____

_____

_____

_____

_____

_____

_____

_____

How can you better gain commitment from the consumer at the commitment stage?

_____

_____

_____

_____

_____

_____

_____

_____

_____

_____

_____

Are you tenacious in your quest for commitment from the customer?

_____

_____

_____

_____

_____

_____

_____

_____

_____

How can you enhance your approach at the commitment stage to develop long-term connections with customers?

_____

_____

_____

_____

_____

_____

_____

_____

_____

_____

_____

_____

_____

Action Steps

- Develop a clear and straightforward communication strategy for the commitment stage.
- Address any last objections or concerns the consumer may have at the commitment stage.
- Ensure a seamless transition to the post-sale connection during the commitment stage.
- Develop a strategy to obtain commitment from the consumer during the commitment stage.
- Be relentless in your quest for commitment from the consumer.
- Use the commitment stage to develop long-term connections with consumers.
- Have a strategy in place for the post-sale relationship to guarantee continuous client happiness and retention.

Taking the Business Relationship to the Next Level

Summary

In this chapter, Jerry Acuff and Jeremy Miner examine the significance of moving the business relationship to the next level. The authors suggest that effective sales professionals must concentrate on creating long-term connections with clients and enhancing the value of such relationships over time.

Key Lesson

- The most effective sales professionals concentrate on developing long-term connections with clients.
- Sales personnel must consistently deliver value to clients to maintain and grow the connection.
- Salespeople must be proactive in discovering opportunities to offer value and strengthen the connection.
- The new model of selling puts a significant focus on relationship-building and enhancing the value of such ties over time.
- Sales professionals who thrive on pushing the business connection to the next level are better suited to achieve long-term success in their professions.

Self-Reflection Questions

Are you focused on developing long-term connections with customers?

_____

_____

_____

_____

_____

_____

_____

_____

_____

_____

How can you develop trust, mutual respect, and shared values with customers?

_____

_____

_____

_____

_____

_____

_____

_____

_____

_____

_____

_____

How do you consistently deliver value to preserve and expand the connection with customers?

_____

_____

_____

_____

_____

_____

_____

_____

_____

_____

_____

_____

How can you enhance your communication and active listening abilities to take the business connection to the next level?

_____

_____

_____

_____

_____

_____

_____

_____

_____

_____

_____

Are you proactive in recognizing opportunities to offer value and strengthen the relationship?

_____

_____

_____

_____

_____

_____

_____

_____

_____

_____

How can you better integrate the new paradigm of selling into your approach to relationship-building?

_____

_____

_____

_____

_____

_____

_____

_____

_____

_____

_____

_____

_____

Action Steps

- Prioritize relationship-building in your sales techniques.
- Focus on creating trust, mutual respect, and shared values with consumers.
- Continuously deliver value to consumers to sustain and grow the connection.
- Improve your communication and active listening abilities to take the business connection to the next level.
- Be proactive in seeking ways to offer value and expand the connection.
- Incorporate the new paradigm of selling into your approach to relationship-building.

Learning Review Questions

Did you achieve your intended goals or objectives as described at the start of this workbook? Why or why not?

_____

_____

_____

_____

_____

_____

_____

_____

_____

_____

_____

_____

_____

_____

In reflecting on your progress throughout the workbook, what were the key strengths you displayed in your learning and personal growth?

_____

_____

_____

_____

_____

_____

_____

_____

_____

_____

_____

_____

_____

_____

What were the most difficult sections or subjects in this workbook for you? How did you overcome such difficulties?

_____

_____

_____

_____

_____

_____

_____

_____

_____

_____

_____

_____

_____

How did this worksheet help you grasp the subject? Did it live up to your expectations in terms of insightful insights and practical application?

_____

_____

_____

_____

_____

_____

_____

_____

_____

_____

_____

_____

_____

_____

Think about the chapter questions and action tasks provided in this worksheet. Which ones did you find most useful, and why? How did you incorporate them into your regular life or routine?

_____

_____

_____

_____

_____

_____

_____

_____

_____

_____

_____

_____

_____

_____

In reflecting on your experience with this workbook, what changes or improvements have you noticed in yourself? How has your perspective, mentality, or conduct changed?

_____

_____

_____

_____

_____

_____

_____

_____

_____

_____

_____

_____

_____

How would you grade the arrangement and structure of this workbook? Was it simple to follow and did it flow logically from one section to the next?

_____

_____

_____

_____

_____

_____

_____

_____

_____

_____

_____

_____

_____

_____

Overall, how would you rate the usefulness of this workbook in assisting you to attain your personal or learning goals? What specific factors contributed to or detracted from its effectiveness?

_____

_____

_____

_____

_____

_____

_____

_____

_____

_____

_____

_____

_____

17829437R00050